Robert M. Hannon

THE TWILIGHT OF SAIL

ROBIN KNOX-JOHNSTON

G. P. PUTNAM'S SONS
New York

First American Edition 1979

Introduction copyright © 1978 by Robin Knox-Johnston

Photographs copyright © 1978 by Popperfoto/Conway Picture Library

Designed by Bob Hall

Front endpaper: The barque *King Malcom* in dry dock at Montevideo, 1896

Back endpaper: Bristol docks in the nineteenth century

Page 1: The *Fortuna* under tow

Pages 2-3: Furling the fore course in a storm aboard the *Garthsnaid*
Page 5: The *Padma* drying her sails

Library of Congress Catalog Card Number: 78-19584

SBN: 399-12307-5

Printed in Great Britain by
The Anchor Press Limited

CONTENTS

For the traveller at the beginning of the nineteenth century an ocean passage basically meant very much what it had meant to travellers 3,000 years before: weeks or months of deprivation and hardship with the likelihood of a death from shipwreck, foundering or disease. Sea and ocean transport had slowly developed over the years, but were still dependent upon the wind in a sail and although Phoenician seamen would have marvelled at the height of the masts, the complexity of the sails and rigging, and the physical size of the ships, the principles of sailing a nineteenth-century ship would have been quite clear to them. Sea transportation had developed over the centuries but it had not been revolutionized.

The Industrial Revolution provided the machinery that slowly, and after overcoming considerable prejudice, began to provide an alternative method of ship propulsion. The early engines were large, inefficient and thoroughly unreliable. They had the added disadvantage that they caused considerable vibration, a hazard because shipwrights had been used to building structures to withstand reasonably even strains from wind and waves which they understood well. Vibration from the early steam engines produced strains that were not understood and for which no compensating strength in their structure existed. The resulting springing of planks and opening of seams hardly endeared this method of propulsion to the seafarers of the time. Within a very short time, however, engineers had turned their minds to the problem and stronger, specially designed wooden vessels began to appear, followed by iron ships held together by rivets instead of nails. Still the engines remained unreliable, and no sober-minded shipowner dreamed of building a vessel without masts and sails as well as steam until near the end of the century. Neither did the sober-minded shipowner like the thought of all that free wind going unused and, as coal for the boilers took up space that could otherwise be profitably used to carry cargo, most steamships were built with sails which their Masters were encouraged to use in preference to the engine.

Pure sailing-ships carried the bulk of world trade for the first half of the nineteenth century and, although the reliability of steamships

The *Procyon* with everything set. Built in 189 and, at 2,132 tons, one of the largest three-masted barques under the British flag, she distinguished herself on her maiden voyag by sailing to New York in fifteen days

6

improved steadily, they were not able to compete economically on the longer trade routes because of the cost of coal and the need for frequent stops to refill their bunkers.

In warships, where considerations of profit and economy do not apply to the same extent, masts and yards for carrying sail were still being rigged right up to near the end of the century, as sail enabled them to cruise greater distances. In one class of cruisers built for the Royal Navy as late as the 1870s it was possible to lower the funnel and raise the propeller so that the ships could sail more efficiently when the wind was suitable. By the 1880s, however, sails, though still carried, were seldom used and naval tactics were revolutionized by the realization that wind direction could be ignored.

The opening of the Suez Canal in 1869 abruptly ended sail's advantages on the Far Eastern routes from Europe and America, and marks the beginning of the real ascendance of steam. The Canal reduced the sailing distance from Europe to the Far East by about 5,000 miles, and it was suddenly possible for steamships to carry cargo more economically on these routes. Even if it used the Canal, no sailing-ship could hope to achieve as fast a passage as a steamship because the winds in the Red Sea were light and unreliable. From this time onwards sailing-ships were forced onto a decreasing number of long routes where the reliability of the wind allowed them to operate as economically as steamers.

It would be wrong to think that the only competition steam had to overcome was the lumbering merchant ships that carried ocean-going trade at the time of the Napoleonic Wars. The century that saw a complete revolution in land transport also saw the development of new, larger and faster sailing-ships.

Initially the improvement was in basic hull design. Ships were lengthened and given finer lines: the customary ratio of beam to length rose from 1:4 to 1:6. Then in 1845 the first of the real clipper ships appeared.

The term clipper had been in general use for some time to describe a fast ship – in particular, brigs and schooners built in Baltimore, and later the fast light vessels of Indian, British or American

The *Eugenie Sneider* with all sail set in a moderate following wind. Despite the size of sail set, the vessel is only moving at a few knots although she is not heavily laden

ownership which ran opium from India to China between 1830 and 1850. All these vessels were built for short fast runs to outpace blockades of one sort or another, and they were usually of no more than 300 to 400 tons, their cargo being of sufficient value to justify its carriage in small quantities.

The *Rainbow*, built in 1845 for a cost of 22,000 dollars, is generally considered to be the first real clipper ship. Although in part evolved from the Baltimore clippers she differed from previous vessels in that her builder gave her a very concave bow and raked stem – what is now called the clipper bow – and this together with her tall masts and large sail-carrying capacity gave her speeds that were previously unheard of. On her second voyage to China she went out from New York and back from Canton in six months and fourteen days. Although the *Rainbow* was lost off Cape Horn in 1848, she more than justified her short life as a model which was developed considerably over the next few years in America and Europe. The clippers' disadvantage of carrying less cargo than previous merchant ships of the same size was not a hindrance at a time when the Californian and Australian Gold Rushes meant that speed earned a premium freight. Any vessel that could almost halve the passage time from the American East Coast or Europe around the Horn to California was guaranteed full bookings.

For a few years these new American Clippers had no rivals on their own routes, but they could not compete on the British foreign markets as the British Navigation Act forbade the carriage of cargoes by any other than British ships. As much as anything, these protective laws had discouraged the building of improved ships by British owners, who were quite content to build slow lumbering cargo carriers as they had no competition. In 1849, however, the Navigation Act was repealed, and the American clippers at once saw their opportunity to move in on the lucrative British tea trade.

The tea trade with China had been a British East India Company monopoly until 1834, and the cargo had been carried in cumbersome ships known as 'tea wagons'. The ending of the monopoly provided opportunities for other British owners, but the tonnage rules governing the tax levied on ships did not encourage the building of sleek vessels.

9

In 1849, after the repeal of the Navigation Act, the *Oriental*, an American clipper, was chartered for the China tea run and completed the voyage from Hong Kong to London in ninety-seven days with 1,118 tons of tea on board. This fast passage caused a great stir at the time and encouraged other American vessels to enter the trade. It well suited the clippers, after a fast run to California, to load ballast and sail for China – a voyage of just over a month – and there load a premium tea cargo, rather than hang around in California for months awaiting a lean cargo for New York. The British could not let the challenge pass and within a year two very fast 'Aberdeen clippers' were launched, which, though smaller, were a match for the larger American ships. These were the *Stornoway* and the *Chrysolite*, which both recorded very competitive maiden voyages.

1851 was the first year that American and British ships competed on the tea run and honours were fairly even.

The excitement caused by these fast voyages, and the international aspect of the competition, attracted tremendous attention. Shipowners began to build ships specifically to win the tea race each year, a factor that led to the development of faster and faster ships. Although in general the British tea clippers were smaller than their American counterparts, they proved just as fast, and the fact that they were built of hardwood, and not American pine, meant that the seams between their planks did not open up as much and so they delivered their cargo in better condition. Either because of this, or because a change in the tonnage rules in 1854 at last encouraged British owners to build faster ships for any trade and not just the premium trades, the Americans disappeared from the China tea races about 1855 and the racing became exclusively British thereafter.

Sailing-ships reached their zenith in the mid 1850s and 1860s on the China run. No faster ocean-going sailing merchantmen had been built before, and after the tea trade began to die in the 1870s nothing to compete was subsequently launched. The prize was the high price that would be fetched by the first tea cargo to arrive in London or New York. Shippers wanted the extra profit and to get it they were prepared to offer bonuses to the

The four-masted barque *Olive Bank* in heavy seas

The *Cutty Sark* rigged as a ship, lying at ancho
in Sydney harbour. Even on the wool trade sh
shows all the smartness of appearance expecte
of a crack ship

shipowner and master of the first ship home. This
was sufficient inducement to shipowners to build
faster ships and employ hard captains to sail them
to their limits.

Agents in China made every effort to get the
cargo into the ships as fast as was humanly possible
once the tea was harvested and packed, and then
the ships would take off for London, some 16,000
miles away.

The course to Europe was south through the
China Sea, via either the Lombok or Sunda Straits
into the South Indian Ocean, and then west to the
Cape of Good Hope. Once round the Cape the
southeast trade winds pushed the ships up to the
equator, where, after drifting through the
doldrums, trimming the sails to every slightest
cat's-paw of wind, they would meet up with the
northeast trade winds which carried them through
the variables about latitiude 30° north. More heavy
work for the seamen and then the ship would pick
up the southwesterlies and race for the English
Channel. Tugs were usually picked up off Dover, as
the race was won by the first vessel to dock in
London, and a ship could lose time trying to sail up
through the Downs and then tack up the River
Thames.

The China tea races were classics in their own
time. Apart from the prize for the captain and crew
of the winning vessel, a great deal of money was
wagered on the outcome of the race each year. The
greatest race took place in 1866, when five ships –
Ariel, Serica, Taeping, Taitsin and *Fiery Cross* –
raced back from Foochow together. Three of them,
the *Taeping, Serica* and *Ariel*, arrived in London on
the same tide and docked within two hours of each
other after a voyage of ninety-nine days.

The only surviving British tea clipper is the
Cutty Sark built for Captain Jock Willis and now
preserved in a dry dock at Greenwich. She was built
expressly to beat *Thermopylae*, commissioned the
previous year, and was almost exactly identical in
her dimensions. Launched at Dumbarton in
November 1869, she took part in eight tea races in
all, but never bettered the earlier record, her fastest
time being 107 days in 1871. She only once raced
Thermopylae but the result was inconclusive as
Cutty Sark lost her rudder in heavy weather in the
Indian Ocean when holding a lead of about 400

miles. The *Cutty Sark* holds the record – 363
nautical miles – for the distance travelled by a
British sailing-ship in twenty-four hours.

The China tea race died after the Suez Canal
was opened in 1869, and the trade was slowly lost to
the steamers. Vessels like *Cutty Sark* were forced
into other trades where they could still compete,
and from 1883 to 1895 she sailed on the Australian
wool run. She recorded some fast passages on this
run, her best being sixty-nine days from Newcastle
in New South Wales, Australia, round Cape Horn to
the Lizard. *Cutty Sark* was sold to Portuguese
owners in 1895 and sailed for them re-rigged as a
barquentine for twenty-seven years until brought
back to the British flag by Captain Downman in
1922. *Thermopylae* similarly traded on the wool run
and her record passage of fifty-nine days from
London to Melbourne, an average of over 10 knots,
still stands for a sailing-ship.

These record runs were considerably better
than the average steam-powered merchant ship of
the day could achieve, and would have still been
competitive with steam in the 1930s. Unfortunately
a sailing-ship could not always guarantee such a
fast passage because of the vagaries of the wind.
Towards the end of the century as sailing-ships had
their rigs cut down to barques and barquentines in
order to cut down on crews and operating costs, they
were no longer capable of such high speeds.

Sail reached its peak with the American ships
racing round the Horn from the American East to
West Coasts, and the China tea races. Both routes
encouraged speed and the ships that were built in
response were the finest wind-powered vessels ever
to sail. But the building of the Suez Canal and the
establishment of a road across the Isthmus of
Panama enabled steamers to move in on these
lucrative routes and brought the great sailing-ship
era to an end. No further developments in
sailing-ship design or operation were possible, and
improvements in steam propulsion were
continually being introduced so that sail had no
chance of regaining a lead.

The common response of a sailing-ship's owner
was to cut his costs as much as he could by keeping
expenses like food and maintenance to the
minimum and by paying as little in wages as
possible. Owners were also forced to search for trade

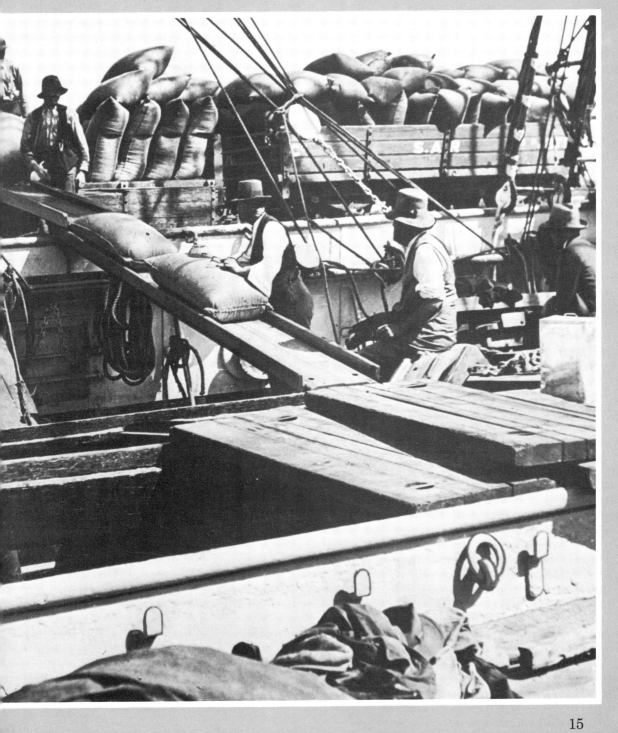

on the longer routes where sail could still compete. The problem was not so much one of finding an outward cargo from Europe to South Africa or Australia – a sailing-ship could make the voyage from Liverpool to Melbourne in about 100 days which was not that much slower than steam– it was the question of finding a cargo from South Africa or Australia once they were there. Apart from wool, coal was one of the few commodities available, and there was no trade in coal to Europe or North America. So a sailing ship might sail out to Durban or Melbourne, Victoria, with a general cargo. This would be discharged and then between 500 and 1,000 tons of stone ballast loaded for the journey to Newcastle, New South Wales. The ballast was necessary because of the weight of the masts, yards and rigging– a sailing-ship's holds could never be completely emptied or she would capsize. Thus when discharging a cargo, a ship would take on part of her new cargo, or ballast, before completely discharging.

On arrival at Newcastle the ship would usually have to wait a month before being able to load and then, when the first 500 or so tons of coal were aboard, she would discharge the stone ballast before filling up with coal. She would then sail to the west coast of South America where the coal would be discharged and, if she was lucky, a cargo of nitrates loaded in the discharge part. If a cargo of nitrates was not available she would have to take on ballast again and head out to one of the guano islands where a cargo of bird manure would be painstakingly loaded by baskets, one at a time. After anything between six and twelve weeks, loading would have been completed and the ship would set sail for Europe around Cape Horn, a voyage of about 100 days.

On arrival in the English Channel, it was usual, unless the winds were fair, to haggle for a tow from the tugs that stationed themselves off Falmouth or, in fair weather, perhaps as far out as the Scillies and even beyond. Few sailing ships sailed into port; they picked up a tug and were towed in. The tugs took their chances, as with no radios no one knew when a ship was to be expected.

A round voyage such as this, which was fairly common, could take anything up to two years. During that time the vessel had earned freight on

A tug hails to offer the *Lingard* a tow at the end of a voyage. Most sailing-ships took tows in and out of port, and even between ports on the European coast

only three cargoes, none of which would carry a premium. This style of business had been acceptable and profitable when the only way to move a cargo was in a sailing-ship, but was increasingly less attractive as steamers became more efficient. A steamer could predict her arrival and book a berth in advance, hence avoiding idle time awaiting a berth. She did not have to load and discharge stone ballast every time she wanted to move as she did not have the weight of mast and rigging to balance. Finally a steamer had steam winches which greatly speeded up cargo handling and thus reduced dock dues. These savings grew greater as steamers became more efficient, forcing freight rates down and making it even harder for sailing-ships to pay their way.

Life on board for the seamen and officers in sailing-ships had always been hard and few improvements in living conditions were added as sail fought to survive. The captain, chief mate and second mate lived aft, with the steward, if one was carried, often sharing a six foot by four foot cabin with the second mate. The apprentices and petty officers such as the bos'n, carpenter and sailmaker lived in a deckhouse on the main deck which often had the galley attached in which the cook worked and slept. The remainder of the crew lived forward in the forecastle.

Most sailing-ships had a low freeboard when loaded, as superstructures were unnecessary windage and got in the way when handling sails. The low freeboard meant that the lee rail of the main-deck bulwarks was frequently under water when the ship heeled over while sailing, and being lower, it was easier for a large wave to sweep on board. In their latter days, the only routes where sail could compete with steamers was on the long hauls down to Australia through the notorious roaring forties where the seas are particularly high, and so a main deck awash was a frequent occurrence. This meant that care had to be taken when any of the weather doors to the accommodation were open or water would sweep in, and many a hot meal was lost between the galley and the poop or forecastle because the crewman carrying the food was swept off his feet by a wave.

Much of the handling of a ship was carried out from the main deck, and with this being frequently

Hands climbing aloft aboard the *Invercauld* a full gale. When loaded down, the decks we nearly always awash in anything above a fres breeze

under water, the seamen were resigned to working up to their waists in sea water. A large wave coming inboard could wash the men into the scuppers and many ships rigged safety nets above the gunwales to 'strain' the men out of a wave that otherwise would have washed them overboard. No seaman's wardrobe carried enough clothing for him to be able to put on dry clothes after many duckings so the men went for weeks on end in rough weather with damp or wet clothing.

The work aloft required nerve and physical strength and stamina. Crawling out on a slippery yard, holding on to a grab rail with one's feet on a foot-rope 150 feet above the deck with the mast swaying around as the ship pitches and rolls, and then grappling with and trying to furl a probably icy sail of heavy canvas, is not a task to be relished by everyone. But the seamen did it as a part of their job, day or night, warm or cold, wet or dry.

Reefing a sail was always an arduous task, the most difficult being the fore or main courses which were the largest sails on board, and often the second mate would lead the men in the job, taking up a position near the middle of the yard and controlling the work from there. It was a matter of pride for the officer to lead the men aloft, but the position of honour was where the work was most dangerous at the yard-arm where the foot-ropes gave a poor foothold. One compensation of working right out at the yard-arm was that if one fell, one fell into the sea with a chance of being picked up. If one fell onto the deck there was little chance of escaping fatal injury.

Securing a large sail in a blow was an incredibly difficult task, and often after an hour spent trying to gather the sail in onto the yard a slight yaw in the course would blow all the sail out again before the gaskets could be secured round it. At times the crew would have to let go of the sail completely and hang on for dear life as the yard would be shaking so much from the effect of the flogging sail. Once a sail was reefed, the hands would climb back down onto the deck and then trim the sail. On most ships all hands would be required to reef a sail and there could be as many as thirty-two sails in the rig. Teamwork was vital if the task was to be completed quickly and safely, but even with a skilled crew much of the night would pass before all sail had been re-trimmed to suit a change of weather.

Reefing or setting sail in the Southern Ocean in a snowstorm with icy foot-ropes and frozen canvas sails was a hazardous enough task and even seamen's hands hardened by constant rough work would become sore and bloody. But there could be no respite, as a man less aloft greatly increased the workload for the remainder, and the safety of all on board depended upon each evolution being carried out as expeditiously as possible.

When not working aloft the crew on watch would be constantly on deck standing by to trim the yards so that the sails were most efficiently aligned to the wind.

All the square sails on a ship were set upon yards – long wood or metal spars supported at the centres by slings which ran from a mast-head and which allowed the yard to be raised or lowered. A truss or parrel was rove from the yard around the mast so that the yard was kept held against it. The square sail was laced at its head along the yard and, at each corner of the foot, sheets were rove which allowed the sail to be hauled in or let out. In order to trim the sail to the wind, tackles, called braces, were rove from the deck to the yard-arms at each end of the yard so that by slacking one brace and hauling on the other the yard could be swung round. In order to trim one square sail, a sheet and a brace would have to be eased out and the opposite sheet and braces hauled in. Although some yards were cross-linked, tacking or altering course generally involved adjusting every square sail. In the trade winds or in a steady blow this work would not occur so frequently, but in calm conditions, such as the variables or the doldrums where the wind is fickle, the crew would work constantly at trimming the sails, which, apart from the frustrating lack of progress, explains why seamen almost preferred rounding the Horn to sailing through the doldrums.

The trade-wind belts gave the sailors their most enjoyable and the doldrums their least enjoyable sailing, but the Southern Ocean gave them their most dangerous moments. In most areas of the world, a squall might be the greatest hazard, the size of the seas being insufficient usually to threaten a well found craft. Down in the roaring forties things were different. The size of the swell

Men hauling on the crossjack braces in moderately heavy weather

waves alone made a ship seem minute, and when a storm came it built up seas that completely dwarfed the ship. In these conditions a ship would run before the wind under lower topsails and storm staysails as long as she could, trying to keep up sufficient speed to keep ahead of the wave crests which would otherwise come over the stern smashing all before them. Often the helmsman would be forbidden to look astern as the sight of these mountainous waves would unnerve even the stoutest seaman and a moment's lost concentration would prove fatal. As the 'Greybeard' approached, the stern would lift and the ship would rush down the forward slope of the wave. This was the most dangerous time for a ship running before a gale because if the rudder ceased to 'bite' the ship could swing round in front of the oncoming crest, or 'broach to', and would then be knocked flat. A ship in ballast would probably founder after such a blow, as not even the stoutest of securings could hold the ballast in place. If the ship were lucky she would have some sail left after being knocked down and would be able to get back on course again. If the sails had been carried away and the wheel or rudder were damaged, her only chance lay in swinging round head to wind so that she could heave to before the waves swept the deck clear and broke the lashings on the hatches.

The condition of the crew on a vessel that had broached can be imagined. Most counted themselves lucky to be alive, but knew that the ship could founder any time and worked for their lives to keep the ship afloat. Often days would pass before it was safe to try to set sail again and during this time no one would expect a hot meal or a dry bed.

If a captain felt that a really bad storm was approaching he would try to heave to before it reached its maximum strength and conditions made swinging the vessel round too dangerous. Often, though, it was difficult to tell whether conditions would deteriorate to the extent that heaving to was desirable, and in that case he could only try to run before the wind and seas and hope that no monster wave appeared.

A barque of 1,500 tons would carry twelve able seamen who were divided into two watches, the mate's and the second mate's watch. At the beginning of a voyage the mate and second mate would choose their watches and these would remain

Below: Furling the fore course in a storm aboard the *Garthsnaid*. Not the task for a person with a weak stomach, but everyday work for a sailor

Right: Men wrestling with a sail on a yard-arm. The foot-rope has been pushed out horizontally as they struggle to gather in the sail

unchanged throughout the voyage unless death or illness intervened. The apprentices were split between the watches and did the same work as the seamen, few if any even taking a sight throughout their apprenticeship. The apprentices served a four-year indenture, for which their parents paid the shipowner £25, and during those four years the apprentice's wages were calculated to equal exactly that sum. The shipowner fed them and provided accommodation and in return had their labour for four years for nothing. After completing the four years, an apprentice was released from his indentures and could sit his second mate's examination, better known as his second mate's ticket. If his indentures expired whilst away on a voyage, he could hope for an uncertified third mate's posting at about £4 a month, or the captain could sign him on as an able seaman for about £3.50 a month.

The watches worked a routine of four hours on and four hours off, changing to two hours a watch during the dog watches. As eight to ten men were insufficient to handle the sails in the event of a squall or tacking, 'All hands' would be called for these tasks and the watch off duty lost their rest. In addition to the work of sailing the ship, the usual routine maintenance and upkeep of the vessel had to be carried out and this was usually done by the off-duty watch during the daylight hours. Sailing-ships rarely carried mechanically powered winches, so all the work of trimming sheets or hauling in the anchor was done by muscle power, sometimes through a hand winch or the capstan. In anchorages or ports where there were no cranes, the crew would help load and discharge the cargo, in addition to the routine work on board. It is small wonder that seamen deserted sail to work on steamers where the deck was seldom under water, there was no dangerous work aloft, steam auxiliary winches were available to help with anchor work and cargo handling, and more regular voyages.

Between working the ship or maintaining her during daylight and being on watch half the night at best, there was little time for pleasure, and even the most insignificant break of the routine became a talking point. The sighting of another ship at sea would bring all hands on deck to help identify her and criticize her rig. The men aboard the slowest

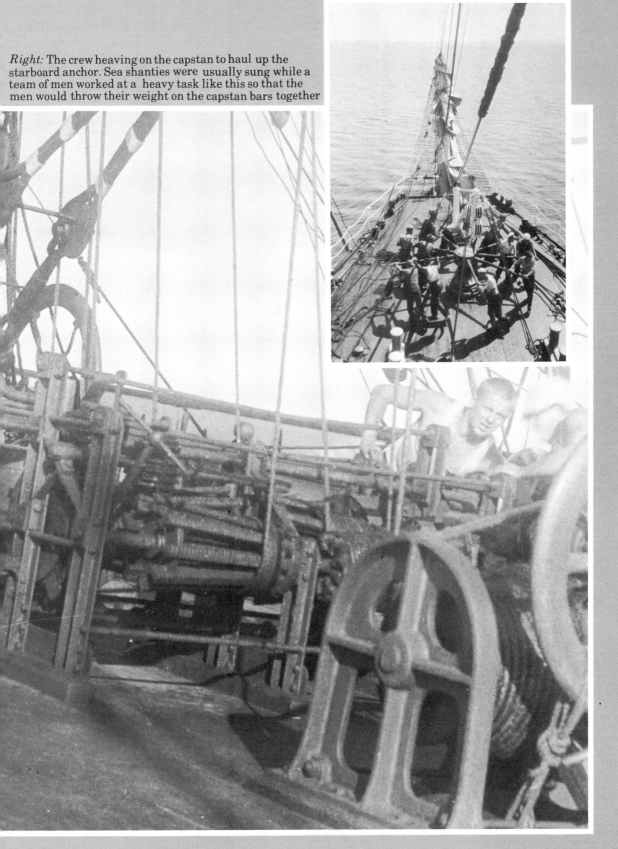

Right: The crew heaving on the capstan to haul up the starboard anchor. Sea shanties were usually sung while a team of men worked at a heavy task like this so that the men would throw their weight on the capstan bars together

and dirtiest of ships would make the most of even the most insignificant good point about their own craft. Any interruption of the back-breaking monotony was welcomed, and such time-honoured traditional ceremonies as initiating a 'first-voyager' when 'Crossing the Line' (the equator) were entered into with enthusiasm, the initiation being a rough and ready affair, much less couth than the frolic provided for entertainment aboard passenger ships. King Neptune and his spouse, carefully chosen from among the crew, would appear over the bow and march aft to greet the captain who would list the newcomers. The attendants would then hunt out the first-voyagers who would be brought before Neptune, tried for such offences as trying to catch flying fish with a broom handle instead of a cricket bat, and sentenced. No one was ever found 'not guilty' and sentences usually consisted of drinking a foul medicine, being shaved – head as well as chin – and then being hoisted aloft in a chair. When the chair was high enough, absolution was given and the chair released so that it fell into a canvas pool. The day was usually rounded off by the captain calling aft all hands to splice the mainbrace. Crossing the Line was a major beano for the crew and excuses for such skylarks were rare.

Sailing-ship men had the opportunity of getting much closer to nature than the crew of a powered vessel. A vessel dependent upon natural forces for her propulsion seems much more a part of nature, and not having the constant vibration of engines or propellers to frighten wildlife away, gives those on board unique views of fish, mammals and birds in their natural habitat. Despite the feeling of sharing the environment with God's creatures, seamen were not particularly superstitious about killing them. Although whales would be avoided because of the damage they could do to the ship, fish were caught and eaten as a supplement to the diet whenever possible.

Sharks were considered fair game by sailors who believed that every shark had killed a poor seafarer, and by killing a shark they avenged a comrade's death. If the captain allowed, a baited hook would be put on a line overside whenever a shark was about and the crew would wait expectantly for the shark to bite. Once the hook had caught, the crew would lay along the line and pull

Father Neptune, his Queen Aphrodite, the court and victims, or those who had not crossed the equator before, photographed on the main deck of the *County of Inverness*. The Crossing the Line ceremony gave the sailors an opportunity to enjoy an official skylark

the shark in. If there was one thing a sailing man was good at it was pulling on a rope, and a crew of a sailing ship would be more than a match for even a large shark. Once the shark was alongside, a noose would be lowered down the line and slipped along the body until it could be tightened round the tail fin. The shark was then hauled on board and cut open to see what the stomach contained, the crew almost expecting to find human remains among the contents. Although shark meat was seldom eaten, the backbone would be cut out and stiffened to make a walking-stick, the jaw-bone and teeth would be mounted as a trophy and the tail fin was usually nailed to the heel of the jib-boom to bring fair winds. Catching a shark gave the crew some excitement and usually pleased the mate as well because the crew would willingly holystone the deck after gutting the shark to clean the mess away.

In Coleridge's *The Rime of the Ancient Mariner*, killing an albatross brought bad luck because the birds were thought to embody the souls of dead sailors, and certainly some seamen believed this to be true. Others were less superstitious, and albatrosses were caught and killed by seamen because catching them provided excitement and the feathers could be used to make a decorative coat. Other parts of the bird were used to make tobacco-pouches and the like. The albatrosses were caught either with a baited hook or on a small triangular baited plate which caught the bird's hooked beak in its apex. Once caught the bird was jerked onto its back and hauled inboard. When on deck an albatross was unable to take off again as the deck of a ship provided an insufficient runway. One does not like to think of these graceful birds being killed just to provide tobacco-pouches but the number involved was probably small.

Most of a crew would be made up of prime volunteers but captains were often forced to bring the numbers up to strength just before sailing by hiring men from crimps, the unofficial suppliers of seamen. Much has been said about the behaviour of the seamen of the day, but they led a hard deprived life, and it is only to be expected that they would let their hair down once they reached port, assuming the captain allowed shore leave. The crimps had no excuse, and it is perhaps one of the greatest criticisms of the authorities of the time that the

Right: Albatross caught and killed aboard t *Loch Tay*. Some seamen were superstitious about killing albatross, but by no means all thought it would bring bad luck

Below: Two crew members aboard the *Loch T* skinning an albatross. The webbed feet wer used to make much-prized tobacco-pouches

crimp was able to survive, and very comfortably, out of selling seamen to a desperate ship's master. The whole foul business was dependent upon their being no surplus seamen available. When this happened seamen from a ship just arrived in port would be enticed into a tavern, drugged, made drunk or knocked out, and then kept hidden away until the crimp had negotiated a good price for seamen for a ship about to sail. The seamen were dumped on board, usually unconscious, and the first they would know was when they were rousted out to help weigh anchor or set sail. Then they would discover which ship they were on, where she was bound and even which nationality she was. The ship was sailing and the last chance of getting back ashore had gone, so the men had no choice but to sign the articles of agreement, which legally bound them to the ship for the duration of the voyage. The only real losers by this system were the seamen, who lost the wages they had earned on the previous ship because they had been forced to desert, and had the crimp's fees deducted from the wages they earned on their next ship.

Discipline on board a sailing ship was necessarily strict. There could be no place for the man who refused to jump to a task when ordered, because a delay could be hazardous to all on board. The officers were obeyed partly because it was illegal to disobey a lawful command, and partly because, in general, they were respected for their professional competence. As all the officers had served at least a four-year apprenticeship they were usually well qualified for their task. There was little the seamen could do about unfair treatment except ask to speak to the captain about it, and the usual way of airing a grievance was for a delegation from the forecastle to ask for a meeting. If the captain refused to listen to the complaint, the seamen had to accept the situation, but a bad captain quickly got a reputation as such, and would find signing on a new crew a difficult task. The ultimate legal action a captain could take with his crew was to clap them in irons and bring them to trial at the next port. He could fine them, but any fines or punishments had to be entered in the log-book and could be investigated by a shipping master – the person responsible for signing a crew on and off the articles of agreement at the end of a

Looking aft from the bowsprit of the *Port Jackson*, making a fair speed with a quarteri wind

voyage – and reversed if necessary. The 'bucko
mate' – the man who hammered the crew into
submission with his fists – certainly existed, but
was a much more common occurrence in the
American merchant marine than any other.
'Belaying-pin soup', or a crack on the head with a
belaying pin was standard fare in American ships.
Captains such as the infamous 'Bully' Waterman
would not have been tolerated in any other fleet. On
his last voyage in command of *Challenge* he could
only attract four English-speaking crew out of a
total of sixty-four men signed on in New York. On
this voyage, four men were killed by the captain –
one of them who had been injured being sewn into
his blanket and tossed overside still groaning –
three of the four English-speaking seamen were
flogged, and the fourth had his arm broken and was
thrown into irons in a ship's boat for half the
voyage. The second mate was drugged and then
given the same treatment. Five more men died of
'sickness' according to the log-book. On arrival in
San Francisco a lynch mob tried to hang the
captain, but he was arrested and eventually stood
trial for murder. Although he bribed his way clear
of the charges, his behaviour was too much for even
American shipowners and he never went to sea
again.

In 1876 Samuel Plimsoll's Act was at last
passed through Parliament in England and the
Board of Trade was given the right to inspect ships
and ensure that they were not overloaded. Shortly
afterwards, rules were introduced regarding the
treatment of the crew and the number of A.B.s that
must be carried. A scale of provisions was also laid
down which removed many of the abuses, but
although sufficient provisions had to be on board
little could be done if they were inedible once a ship
had gone to sea.

The Board of Trade had laid down a basic
provisioning scale known to seamen as the 'pound
and pint' because these two words appeared
frequently in the scale – 'Three-quarters of a pound
of salt beef or half a pound of pork, a pound of bread
or a hard biscuit and three quarts of water per day'.
Some of the water, about a third, was taken as the
cook's whack and used by him for cooking. The scale
included a set amount of butter, jam, and sugar or
molasses, usually issued on 'whack' day once a

31

week. At the start of a voyage a certain amount of fresh food was taken aboard, but this did not last longer than the first week or so and from then on the crew were fed on salt food until they reached port. Shipowners mistrusted accounts that included items for provisions as they thought that the captain might be taking a profit on the side. The result of this was that captains wishing to impress their owners would avoid buying any fresh food, and salt stores taken on at the beginning of a voyage of nearly two years might have to last the whole voyage. Inevitably, the stores went bad, but there was little a crew could do about it, and they had to make do with rotten food or starve, and a man who spent his life in hard physical labour was usually hungry.

In 1903 the captain of the *County of Pembroke* underestimated how long it would take to load his cargo of guano. The result was that the crew ran out of food completely except for weevily ship's biscuits, and were forced to obtain provisions from a passing steamer in the North Atlantic. No attempt had been made to call in and buy supplies on the voyage up from the Horn despite a delegation from the crew, and if the crew had taken the matter any further they would have risked imprisonment for mutiny. They were literally forced to starve or hang, the law gave no alternatives if the captain remained stubborn.

Fortunately, few captains behaved in this manner, and most tried to obtain good provisions. But there was no means of refrigerating food, and expensive tinned meat or salted meat from a barrel were the only alternatives. Vegetables would last only as long as they could be kept dry. So it was difficult to provide good food for the whole of a three- or four-month voyage and most sailing men accepted this fact philosophically. The use of limes as an anti-scorbutic was widespread and so cases of scurvy were not the inevitable consequence of such a poor diet as they would have been 100 years before.

Once a ship left port on a voyage she was out of touch with the rest of the world. Without wireless telegraphy, the only method of reporting was either to pull into port – but this was avoided if at all possible – or to 'speak' to another ship and rely on the exchange being reported by both ships when

Burial at sea. With small crews, the loss of a shipmate was keenly felt both because of the loss of a companion and because of the extra work for the rest of the crew

33

they reached their destinations. 'Speaking' to a ship meant exchanging signals, either with flags or by megaphone if the ships got close enough to each other. In sail, in the days when accidents were fairly common through fire, stranding or dismasting, such reports were invaluable to the merchants and provided much needed reassurance to relatives of the crews on board. It is a horrendous fact that a new sailing ship had as much chance of finishing her life on the casualty list at Lloyd's as she did of being broken up, and the description 'Overdue – presumed lost' was all too familiar to those involved in shipping.

In the last thirty years of sailing-ships, most of the men who signed on ship's articles did so out of a pride in being a sailing-ship man. They looked down on the seamen aboard the steamers, and considered them less professional and not real seafarers. As the gap between the living and working conditions aboard sailing-ships and steamers widened, the pride of being a sailing-ship man perversely increased.

The natural hazards at sea were an accepted part of a sailor's life. Wrecking on a shore took the heaviest toll mainly because it was difficult before the days of radio time signals to be sure of the ship's longitude. The calculation of longitude depends on knowing the time accurately – an error of a second can mean that the calculated position is a mile out. In a voyage of 100 days or more accumulated errors could mean that a captain's estimate of his position was wildly out and the ship could pile up on a shore before any land was expected.

Headlands, such as the Lizard in Cornwall, just off the port of Falmouth, took a heavy toll. Ships would use the Lizard as a landfall and in storms or poor visibility an error of a mile made the difference between a safe rounding of the headland and disaster. The Lizard took more than its fair toll of wrecks as there is deep water close up to the rocks and so a captain would not even be warned that he was too close by taking soundings.

Calculating a dead-reckoning position, which meant deciding where a ship was by plotting the course steered and the distance covered from the last known position, gave only a rough idea of the ship's true position. It could not take into account such outside factors as the wind and current.

The *Hansey* wrecked at the Lizard in 1911. H deck cargo of timber has been thrown onto t rocks

Heaving the log, the only method of finding th
speed of a ship before the introduction of pater
logs. Note the sand-glass for timing

Nevertheless, it gave some idea and the log was streamed out every watch, or in some cases every hour, so that the ship's speed through the water was known. Streaming the log meant dropping into the water a piece of wood attached to a long line which was marked every 100 feet. A sand-glass which timed a minute was turned and the line paid out. At the end of the minute the log line was held and the number of marks that had been paid out was the speed of the ship in knots.

Apart from the log-line and his sextant and chronometer, the captain, who usually did all the navigating himself, had no other aids to position-finding, apart from the lead line, the sharp eyes of the lookout, and his knowledge of the seas he was in– certain seas are identifiable by their colour, and the swell alters perceptably as the sea becomes shallower. The moment visibility fell through fog or bad weather, a captain would have to navigate entirely by dead reckoning, and if he had not an accurate position for some time, the vessel could be anything up to fifty miles away from where she was expected to be. Small wonder that vessels piled up on headlands like the Lizard, where, in many cases, they were less than two miles from safe water.

The *Cromdale*, wrecked in 1913, is typical. Thick fog had prevented the captain from taking sights or bearings for a number of days as the ship closed Falmouth 126 days out from Chile with a cargo of nitrates. A steamer passing close by gave the captain the impression that he was on a safe course, but a few minutes later the vessel went aground off Bass Point close to the Lizard lighthouse. The ship was badly holed and settled quickly, and lying in such an exposed position was soon broken up by the sea. The crew escaped, thanks to a prompt response by two lifeboats and helped by the calm weather. The *Cromdale* and her sister ship the *Mount Stewart* were built in 1891 and were the last ships specifically built for the Australian wool trade.

Sailors wrecked off an inhabited shore of a civilized country could count themselves fortunate. Life-saving organizations existed, trained to rescue shipwrecked sailors either with lifeboats or by means of a breeches-buoy. The only chance for those wrecked upon an uninhabited coast lay in the ship's own boats, and if a ship ran ashore in foul weather,

launching the boats might be impossible. Not every crew were as lucky as those aboard the *Glencairn* in 1907. This four-masted barque hit a sandbank off the Horn. A boat was launched but it capsized drowning two of the crew. The rising tide floated the ship off and she drifted for several days while the crew fought a losing battle with the pumps. Eventually when the main deck was awash, the crew took to the boats again and tried to find somewhere safe to land. Fires lit by the local inhabitants attracted them towards the only safe bay in hundreds of miles, but not before two of the crew had died from exposure in the freezing temperatures. Once safely ashore, the survivors were still several days' journey from the nearest settlement but they eventually reached safety after a couple of weeks.

Few crews in difficulties off the Horn got off as lightly as that of the *Glencairn*. An amazing escape was made by the crew of the four-masted barque *Andrina* in 1899. In misty weather she went aground in Policarpo Cove on the north coast of Tierra del Fuego, but because of the strong swell the crew were unable to launch the boats, and were eventually rescued by local inhabitants after being aground for over two months. The story does not end there, however. The cove protected the ship from further damage and she was eventually refloated and salvaged nineteen years later.

Most ships took the Cape Horn route out to the American coast because it was shorter than going the easier way round the Cape of Good Hope through the Indian and Pacific Oceans. Few of the hard-driving sailing-ship captains would have risked their reputations by taking the longer, easier route anyway. In 1895 the choice of routes was put to the test. Two ships, the *Trafalgar* and the *Fairport* both outward bound, found themselves becalmed within a few hundred feet of each other in the doldrums, and the captains had a private bet on which ship could reach San Francisco first using the different routes. The *Trafalgar* set out east and after a stop of twenty-seven days in Sydney eventually reached San Francisco a week ahead of her rival, who had, it must be admitted, a rather slow passage.

Cape Horn's fearsome reputation is based upon some chilling wrecks and disasters, and the fact

The *Reliance* on fire in Iquique, Chile. Once a fire aboard had started, a bucket chain was the only method of fire fighting a ship had. If she was lucky and was in port, other ships would send fire-fighting parties

that it was the scene of a disproportionate number of sailing-ship losses. The Southern Ocean is the only area of the world where the wind and sea can drive right round the globe without touching land. This continuous uninterrupted flow allows huge waves to build up, waves that often exceed sixty feet in height but can sometimes be 120 feet high. Cape Horn marks the southernmost penetration of land into the Southern Ocean, some 700 miles further south than New Zealand. But 600 miles off the south of Cape Horn lies the northernmost part of Antarctica, Graham Land. Into this gap is funnelled the wind and water that can normally spread itself out over 2,000 miles of emptiness. The result is violent winds and currents, and seas that are heaped up and more dangerous than anywhere else in the world. Few sailors approach the Horn without trepidation. The usual and safer rounding is made from West to East, but ships bound from Europe to the American West Coast beat round from East to West, and considered themselves exceedingly fortunate if they made the passage without incident. In the 1905 season, one of the worst years on record, of 130 sailing vessels that went from Europe to the American West Coast via the Horn, only fifty-two reached their destinations without major trouble. By July of that year, when few ships would even dare to reach that latitude let alone attempt a rounding, four were known to have been wrecked, twenty-two were in port for major repairs, and forty-nine were unaccounted for.

The Welsh shipowners, Robert Thomas and Company, owned some thirty-six sailing-ships at one time or another. Of these vessels five were sunk by enemy action in the First World War, eleven were posted missing or wrecked, and nine were known to have been lost off Cape Horn.

By the beginning of the twentieth century, although there were still many sailing vessels about, fewer were being built, shipowners preferring the greater security that a powered vessel gave them. Apart from the run around the Horn from Australia, which was still the preserve of sail as few steamers could take the enormous strains on their engines in rough weather when the propeller was one minute thrashing in the air and the next biting suddenly into deep water, sailing ships were losing out all over the world to steamers.

The *Killoran* airing her sails whilst a cargo is being loaded

40

To give some idea of the numbers of sailing ships still about it is worth mentioning that during the Boer War the British War Department chartered nearly 200 sailing-ships to carry stores out to South Africa, and at one time nearly 150 were anchored off Capetown alone waiting their turn to discharge. This number does not, of course, reflect the proportions of sailing-ships to steamers involved: sailing-ships cost less to keep at anchor than steamers and so took second place in the queue for berths.

The gradual switchover from sail to steam presented few problems for the seamen, many of whom, and particularly the officers, were still encouraged to complete their training under sail as it was felt that sail gave a man a better understanding of the sea, and if he could handle a sailing-ship he could handle any ship. This attitude has persisted right up to the present day, and there are still full-rigged sailing-ships in use in some countries for training young officers. But the sail training ship was appearing at the beginning of this century, when it was realized that berths for apprentices were becoming fewer as the sailing fleets declined, and efforts were made to ensure that this unique grounding in all the arts of seamanship survived.

Although most shipowners picked up the cargoes they could with their large, well tried economical barques, some attempted to produce ships that could still compete directly with power. The German Flying 'P' Line produced the largest full-rigged ship ever built, the *Preussen* which was unfortunately wrecked early on. But with her five masts and acres of square sails she had to carry a large crew. Larger square-rigged ships could not be built as it was physically impossible for men to handle sails on yards of any greater size, so the *Preussen* represents the upper limit in size that could be reached by square rig, and even then she was only marginally competitive with the steamers of her day.

One of the most interesting attempts to cut the operating costs of sailing ships was the seven-masted American schooner, *Thomas W. Lawson*. Built towards the end of the nineteenth century at Quincy, Massachusetts, she measured 5,000 tons gross and had a waterline length of 385 feet. Her seven masts were each 193 feet high and carried nothing but fore and aft sails. All her halyards, topping lifts and sheets were led to two steam winches, one on the forecastle and one aft. Because of the lack of square sails all her sails could be set, furled and reefed from the deck, and the powered winches meant that only sixteen men were required to handle her enormous sail area. She was unfortunately lost off the Scilly Isles in 1907 with only one survivor, and no other attempts were made to build labour-saving ships of this type. The principles involved in the *Thomas W. Lawson* came closest to creating a competitive sail-powered alternative to steam propulsion, and are still being investigated today.

Despite their lessened competitiveness against improving powered vessels, sailing-ships would probably have continued to carry a fair proportion of the world's trade well into the twentieth century if two events had not occurred in 1914: the opening of the Panama Canal and the outbreak of the First World War.

The Canal through the Isthmus of Panama meant that a steamship could sail to Europe from Australia or to Europe from the American west coast without having to round Cape Horn. In addition to cutting out this hazard, the distance was reduced by thousands of miles. To compete, sailing ships had to leave the roaring forties where they could guarantee a fast voyage and head up for the doldrums if they were to use the Canal. The Panama Canal did for the Australian and American routes what the Suez Canal had done for the Indian and Chinese trades forty years before, but now there were no other routes for the sailing-ships to fall back on.

The Great War of 1914–18 was the first truly global war, and its effects were felt far from the centres of the conflict in Europe and the Middle East. At the outset, the Germans had a squadron of warships in the Far East which immediately began to search for and sink commercial shipping. Although this squadron sank only six sailing-ships before it was annihilated at the Battle of the Falkland Islands, the fact that its position was unknown forced many ships to remain in port for safety, and sailing-ships, with their dependence on the wind, were unable to dash from port to port as

The *Thomas W. Lawson*, the largest schooner ever built, required a crew of only sixteen men to handle her

could the steamers. Sail in fact contributed to the destruction of the German squadron: while rounding the Horn on their way to attack the Falkland Islands, the Germans captured the American-registered ship, *Drummuir*. Two days were spent stripping the ship and transferring her cargo of coal, and the Germans arrived at the Falklands six hours after the arrival of a superior British squadron. It is interesting to speculate on what would have been the outcome had the *Drummuir* not intervened: it is likely that the German squadron would have discovered that an enemy force was approaching and would have had time to escape.

Three sailing-ships actually witnessed the Battle of the Falkland Islands. They found themselves unwittingly in the battle zone as they made their way north from Cape Horn, but all escaped unscathed.

Sailing-ships were too easy a prey to power-driven surface ships and submarines, and their comparatively slow speed and dependence upon the weather for both course and speed made them impossible to escort. They were no more spared than any other cargo carrier in a total war. Replacement shipping built during the War was entirely power driven, and by the War's end when trade began to get back to normal again, the flood of mass-produced steamers looking for trade quickly pushed aside the depleted sailing fleets.

All over the world creeks and harbours filled with ships that could no longer compete, and they slowly rotted away or were sold to the ship-breakers. A few traded on through the twenties and thirties run by owners who tried to compete, but the Great Depression forced them to give up. Only one shipowner survived through to the forties, a Finn, Gustav Erikson, who as everyone else sold off their great ships bought them up and kept them trading on the Australian and South American grain routes to Europe. He based his fleet at Maarianhamina, a small port in Finland.

Square-rig survives, but only in the dozen or so sail training ships kept going to provide young trainee seamen with the finest basic training in seamanship. Rare glimpses of these 'tall ships' is all that remains to remind us of an epoch that has so recently passed.

The *Ellen* under tow

UNDERWAY

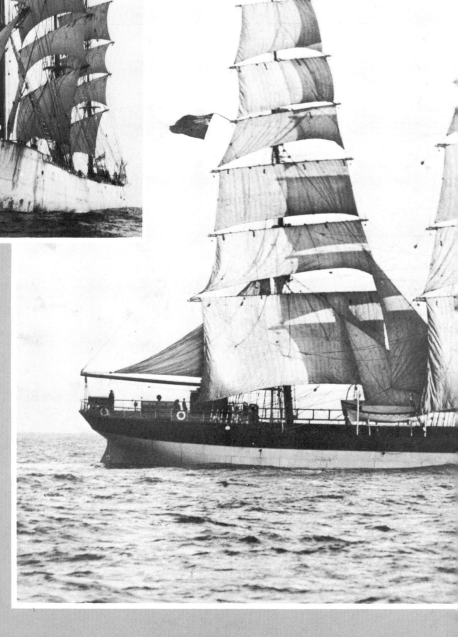

Above: The *Grace Harwar*. Built in 1899 for W. Montgomery and sold to the Russians in 1913. She was subsequently bought by Gustav Erikson and was the last full-rigged ship to be solely employed as a cargo ship

Right: The *Largiemore* close reaching on port tack. A typical example of the last full-rigged ships

Previous pages: The *Ponape*, a four-masted barque, close reaching on starboard tack. A slightly bigger sea would make the decks a wet place to work

Above: The *Maccabeo*, a wooden three-masted barque in light winds off Ailsa Craig

Left: Eliezer leaving port. The upper topgallant sails have not been bent onto their yards, and the anchor has still to be hauled up to the cathead

Right: The wooden barque *Naja* coming into harbour clewing up her lower topsails. When she reaches her anchorage she will come up head to wind, let go the anchor and then lower her upper topsails

Above: The barque *Vardoen* in ballast off Risör, Norway

Right: Eurasia sailing in ballast, which would probably be stones. The necessity of ballasting sailing-ships even when moving them across a dock was one factor that made them uneconomic

ft: The four-masted barque
rnadale, built in 1889, sailing up
Port Phillip Heads, Victoria,
stralia, with a cargo from
gland

ght: The Norwegian brig *Ispolen*.
e was built in 1865 and used to
rry ice to the U.K. She was
ecked in 1893

low: The *Independence*, a
aceful full-rigged ship with
erything set in light weather

Top: The small barquentine *Elizabeth McLea*, close-hauled

Above: The three-masted barque *White Pine* with a bone in her teeth

Right: The barque *Fred*. Note the gaff sail on the mainmast which made her a 'jackass barque'

Left: The three-masted barque *Raupo*. The false gun-ports painted on her hull were a fairly common decoration even at the beginning of the twentieth centu

Below: The barquentine *Elizabethia*, typical of the small craft that traded right up to the middle of the twentieth century

The four-masted barque *Elginshire* in the variables. The variables, or horse latitudes, at the northern edge of the northeast trade winds, meant hard work for the sailors as the sails had to be trimmed to every slight zephyr

The ship *Flottbek* with courses furled in the vicinity of Cape Horn

Left: The *Dovenby*. The sails show the amount of patching that was always a feature of sailing-ships. Most ships carried a specialist sailmaker, but all hands were expected to be able to sew sails if necessary

A remarkably clear photograph taken from the poop looking forward aboard a sailing-ship running with the wind in a quartering sea

63

The *County of Kinross*, one of the famous County Line ships

The steel three-masted barque *Lingard* homeward bound. Built in 1893, she is now on exhibition in Oslo

Right: The barque *Harold* under tow and heeled over to port

Left: The *Port Jackson*, a fully rigged sail training ship torpedoed and sunk in 1917. Although at that time sail was dying in the competitive trades, its value was (and still is) appreciated for training seamen

Above and right: The *C. B. Pederson*, a Swedish four-masted barque used for training. The *C. B. Pederson* traded between Australia and Europe, the trainees learning their seamanship while trading

Left: The five-masted barque *København* built at Leith, Scotland, in 1921 as a trainin
ship.

Right: The Swedish barque *Viking* showing
her identification during the Second World
War

The barque *Beatrice* bound for London with wool from
Australia in 1930

Herzogin Cecilie leaving Falmouth for Birkenhead after a grain race.
Although there was no premium on grain cargoes, the rivalry between
the ships equalled that of the China tea races

The *Herzogin Cecilie* from her port side. The diagonal marks on the
courses are caused by the sails rubbing against their mast forestays

The *Herzogin Cecilie* heeled right over in the North Sea in 1929. The remains of the sails can be seen hanging on to the stays

The *Herzogin Cecilie*. When studding sails ceased to be rigged, extra sails were added on. This photograph shows, from the bottom, the course, lower topsail, upper topsail, lower topgallant, upper topgallant and royal on the foremast

Left: A three-masted barque, showing the stumpy masts and cut-down rig which resulted from the shipowner's efforts to reduce costs and crews

The steel-hulled barquentine *City of Sydney*, built to be handled by a small crew and typical of the ugly attempts to keep sail competitive

Right: A barque in light weather. The hull shows the lack of maintenance, which was skimped in order to save money at the end of the sailing-ship era

Above: A topsail schooner 'doubled'! The *Carl Vinnen* also had an auxiliary engine. It is this type of vessel that came nearest to making sail a competitive form of propulsion. The fact that the ship could motor through the calms, and needed only a small crew, meant that she could give a reasonably accurate arrival date and was quite cheap to operate. If sail is ever to return, ships will have to be built along these lines

Left: The ship *Cunda*, still trading in the 1950s

Right: The four-masted barque *Metropolis* in Norwegian colours during the Second World War

Below: A six-masted schooner. These vessels required fewer crew than a vessel with square sails and were another attempt to keep sail competitive with steam

Below right: The *Brooklands*, a typical coast topsail schooner built as the *Susan Vittery* in Dartmouth in 1859 and still trading at the beginning of the Second World War under the Irish flag

The only five-masted full-rigged ship ever built, the *Preussen*, which was built in 1902. She set a total of forty-seven sails which added up to a sail area of 50,000 square feet

The *Preussen*

The barque *Lawhill* in Swedish colours. She was one of
the last four square-rigged sailing vessels to trade
commercially

The *Lawhill*, photographed as she left Spencer Gulf,
South Australia, with a cargo of 56,000 bags of wheat for
Beira, Mozambique, in March 1948

The training ship *Christian Radich* hailing the *Pamir* on her last
voyage from Australia

Right: The *Pamir* arriving at Falmouth carrying 4,200 tons of grain at the end of her last voyage from Australia

A classic photograph. The
three-masted barque *Shakespeare* and
the 'J' class yacht *Shamrock V* in the
1930s

THE SAILOR'S LOT

Previous pages: About to furl the main course on the *Rodney*. The sail is being clewed up

Right: The carpenter – chippy – caulking a seam on the main deck of the *Beatrice*. It was the carpenter's job to see that the decks and hull remained watertight. On the main deck a spar is laid out for repairs

Below: A seaman splicing a wire. The way he has allowed the strands to fray indicates his lack of experience

The captain, mates, apprentices and the steward of the *Sarata* pictured on the poop deck. Note the captain's dog on deck. Captai[n] frequently took pets to sea with them before t[he] days of animal quarantine

Looking forward on the *Garthsnaid* in a moderate breeze

View of the forecastle of the *Invercauld*. Note the deal wind holes in the foresail, the theory being that allowing air through the sail increased its power

Above: The sailmaker and assistants at work. Most sails were made on board, and any damaged sail would be repaired by the sailmaker, assisted by other members of the crew. Old canvas sails were used in light weather, the new sails being reserved for rough conditions like the Horn

Left: The maze of rigging on a sailing-ship, each piece of which is essential to the smooth and efficient control of the sails. Although it looks incredibly complicated, each function was soon picked up by the 'first voyager'

An albatross trapped on deck. Sailors often caught them, and once on
deck they did not have sufficient space to take off again

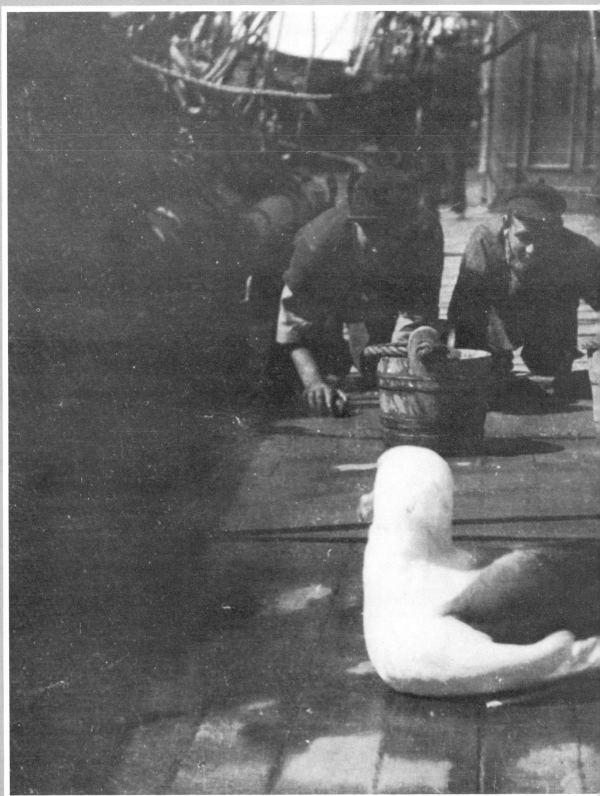

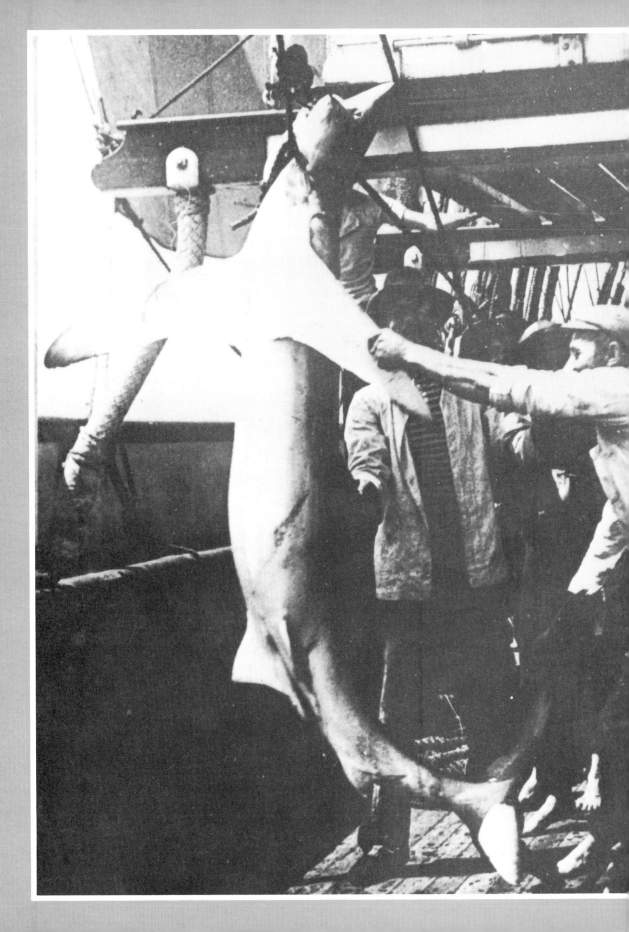

Above: A barracuda caught by one of the crew of the *Loch Tay*. It would be cooked and eaten to supplement the salt meat normally served out to the crew

Left: Sailors hauling a shark inboard on the *Inverclyde*. The tail would be nailed to the job-boom to bring up a wind, the backbone made into a walking-stick, the teeth cut out and mounted as a souvenir, and the skin, shagreen, used as an abrasive. Sailors always examined the contents of the stomach with interest, believing that all sharks had killed some honest seafarer and searching for evidence. By killing a shark they revenged the dead seafarer

The saloon on the Orient Line sailing-ship *Harbinger* built in 1876 for the Australian passenger service. The large object in the middle of the saloon is the mizen-mast

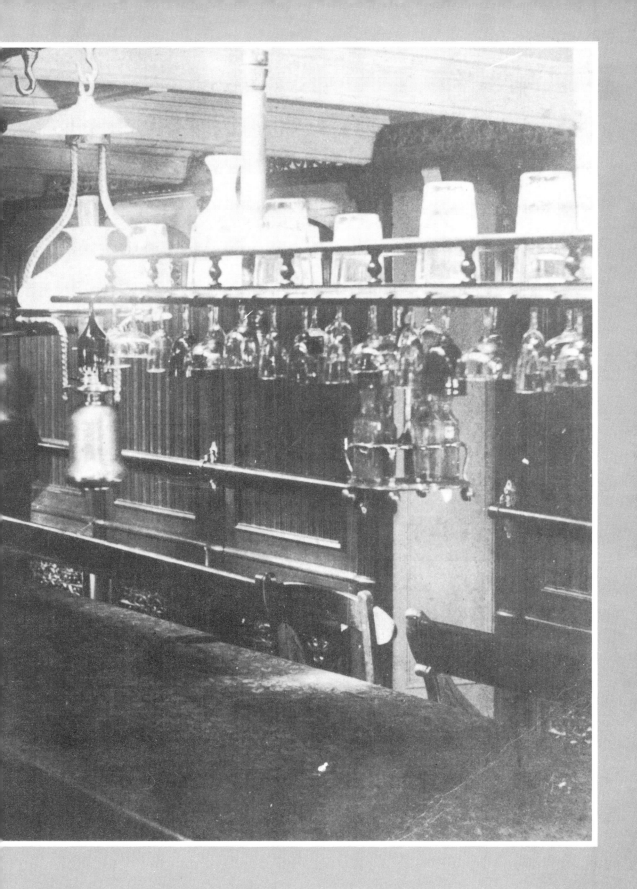

Passengers playing deck quoits the poop of the *Germanic*

Passengers sitting in deck-chairs on the poop. Although allowed on deck in fine weather, passengers were encouraged to keep to their cabins or the saloon when things became rough

Sailors scurrying aloft to let out more sail

Sailors at work on the yard furling a sail on the *Garthsnaid*

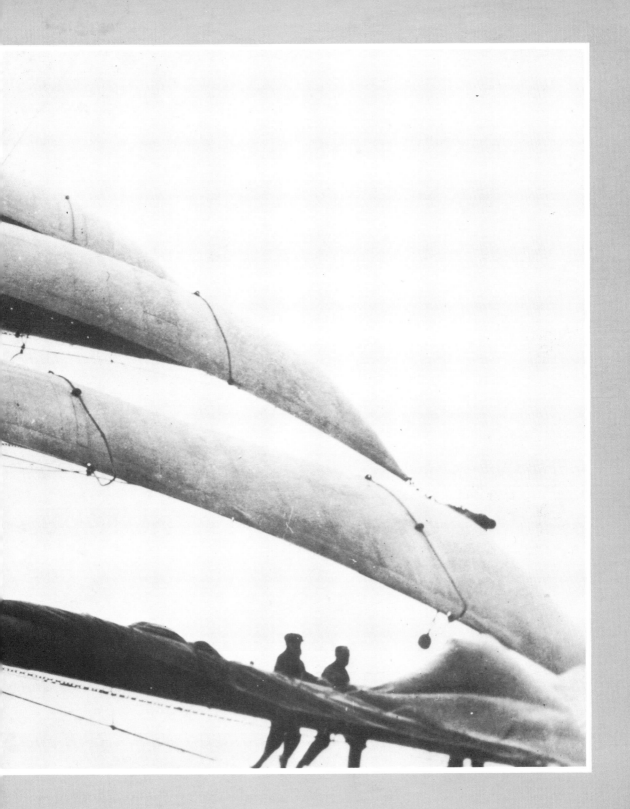

The *Terra Nova* taking Captain Scott on his ill-fated expedition to the South Pole, heeled over before a quartering wind

The *Terra Nova*, looking forward from the poop under full sail

Right: Men at work on deck aboard the *Terra Nova* in the Southern Ocean in a gale

Men hauling on the lee fore-braces

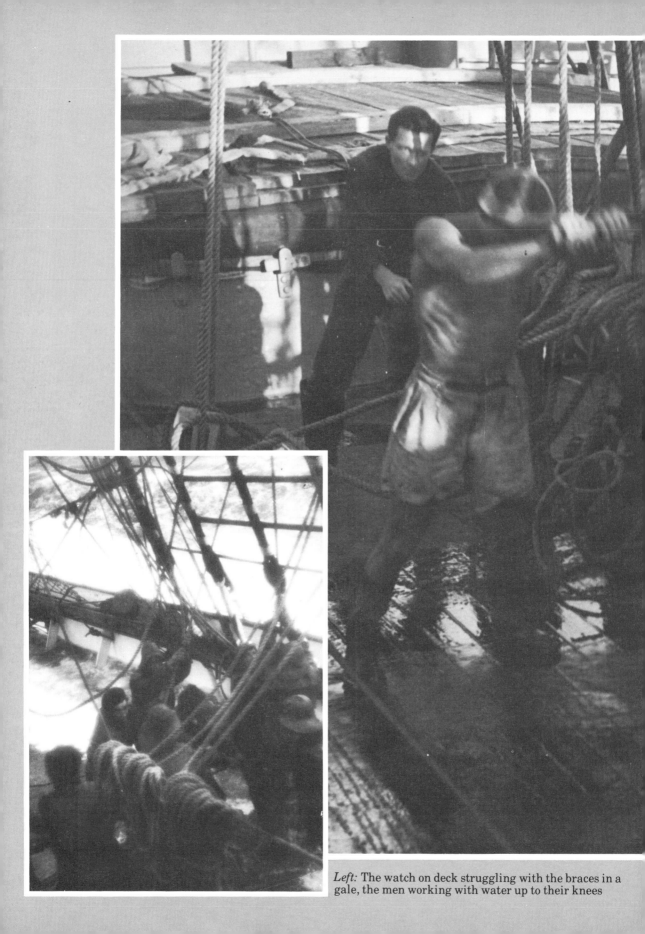

Left: The watch on deck struggling with the braces in a gale, the men working with water up to their knees

Seamen manning the hand pumps to pump out the bilges

The decks awash as the crew hang on to anything to avoid being washed along the deck. Note the lifelines and the net rigged above the gunwale as a guard against seamen being washed overside

A sea rolling aboard the *Invercauld*. If a seaman did not either leap up the rigging or lash himself firmly, this sort of sea could quickly carry him overside and the chances of recovery were slight.

The main deck of the *Garthsnaid* in rough weather. No one on board
was able to keep dry and work the ship in these conditions

Right: A wave breaking against the hull is responsible for this cloud of spray. Note the lifelines and the running rigging turned up on it to prevent the ropes going overside

The mainmast of the *Pamir* with all sail set – over 10,000 square feet of canvas

Two men on the wheel in a strong following sea. Intense concentration was required, and the slightest lapse risked the vessel broaching and being knocked over on to her beam ends by the next wave

Opposite: The wheel lashed together after being smashed in a storm. The helmsman at the time was probably badly injured

126

Previous pages: Vessels in dock at Salthouse, Norfolk, in 1895

Below: The *København* (left) and *Fortuna*. The *København* disappeared in 1928 and none of her crew, including a large number of Danish naval cadets, were ever found

The *København*'s figurehead, carved in teak, represents
Absalom, the warrior who founded the city

Above: The *Cutty Sark*, re-rigged as a ship and in use as a training vessel in Falmouth harbour in the 1920s

The *Shakespeare* being towed into Cape Town docks during the Second World War

131

Sailing-ships waiting to discharge war stores in Cape Town in 1902. At
one time there were nearly 150 sailing-ships waiting to get alongside
and many had to wait more than six months for their turn

133

ft: Ships at anchor in Sydney at the
ginning of the twentieth century. Note the
eat length of the spars, which was made
ssible by the use of tubular steel instead of
ood

Below: Ships loading and discharging in
Geelong, Victoria, Australia, in 1882

Shipping in Wellington, New Zealand,
in the early twentieth century

Merchant shipping at Lyttleton in New
Zealand in 1899. Six out of the eight ships are
pure sailing-ships

Right: Sailing-ships at anchor in San Francisco Bay in 19

Sailing vessels at Pisagua, Chile, in 1890. All the cargo had
to be taken out in lighters and then loaded into the ships by
hand

Inset: Ships awaiting a cargo of nitrates on the Chilean
coast. This was one of the last trades open to sailing-ships,
but ceased to be profitable once the Panama Canal was
opened

Shipping at anchor in the Downs, off Kent, at the end of the nineteenth century. Many ships waited in the Downs for pilots or orders

*t: The *Cape Wrath* adjusting her tow-line. The tug's stern is
*rtly visible on the left. Most sailing-ships were towed round
*m port to port in Europe by the beginning of the twentieth
*atury

Left: The barque *Oaklands* having just taken a tow. The sails have only been clewed up and have yet to be furled properly

The barque *Valparaiso* under tow into port

Right: The *Pacifique* under tow; note that she has the topsails set to help the tug

The *Olgar* under tow

Inset: The *Atlantique* painted up under tow at the beginning of a voyage

Left: The *Lady Isabella* loading coal in Cardiff. Built of iron in 1882, she was lost in the Clyde twenty years later

Sailing-ships moored at Risör, Norway, in 1903

Left: The wooden barque *Hada*, built in 1877, lying awaiting a cargo in the 1920s

Below: Shipping in the port of Antwerp in 1895. Apart from the tugs, no steamers are visible

Left: Pisague drying sails whilst awaiting a cargo

Below: The *Mona* drying sails in Antwerp. Note the broken bowsprit, not an unusual occurrence with this vulnerable spar

The *Wanderer* at anchor awaiting a berth to discharge.
Note the bridge amidships from which the ship was
controlled instead of the more traditional raised poop

Above: The five-masted barque *Potosí* alongside in Hamburg having completed discharging cargo

Above: The French sailing tanker *Quevilly* built in 1897 and the first sailing-ship built to carry petroleum in bulk

The new barque *Willscot* under tow from the builder's yard

157

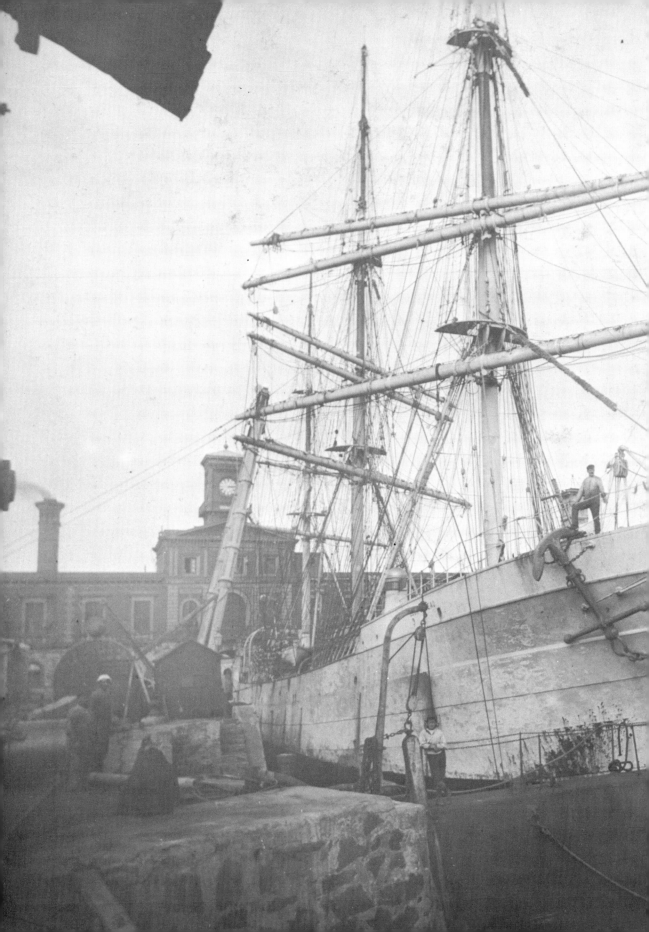

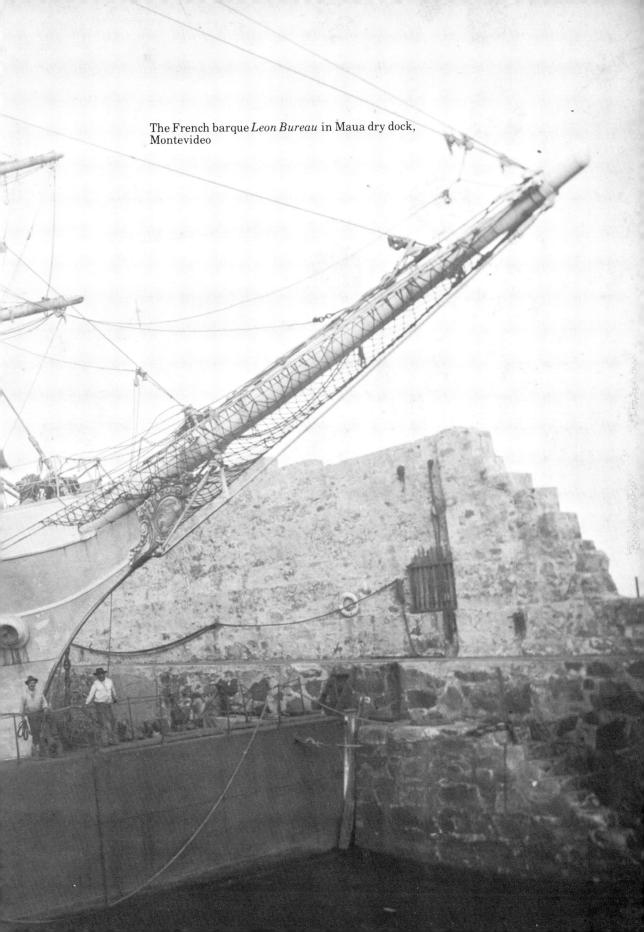

The French barque *Leon Bureau* in Maua dry dock, Montevideo

The American barque *C. D. Bryant* hove down for repairs at Colón, Panama, in 1920. She developed a leak while carrying a cargo of nitrates from Iquique, Chile, to Trinidad via the Panama Canal and put into Colón for repairs

The *Titania* in dry dock. Note the copper sheets nailed onto the bottom of the wooden hull as protection against worms and fouling

The *Crown of Germany* in dry dock. This photograph shows her full lines, indicating her owner's desire for a large cargo rather than speed. Built in 1892 she could carry 3,700 tons of cargo. Sold to German owners in 1910 she was wrecked the same year

The *Fairy Belle* in dry dock

Gustav Erikson's fleet at anchor in Maarianhamina, Finland. This Swedish captain bought up sailing ships as others turned to steam and ran a large fleet right up to the Second World War. The ships in the photograph are, from left to right, the *Viking, Pommern, Olive Bank,* and *Penang*. The bowsprit in the foreground belongs to the *Herzogin Cecilie*

The *Daylight* laid up in Oakland Creek, California, in 1923

The Alaska Packers' Association fleet of sailing-ships laid up in Oakland Creek, California, in 1923. Few of these ships ever sailed again and most were destined for the ship-breakers

WRECKS

Above and right: The *Glenbervie* hard on the rocks at Coverack, Cornwall, in 1899

Previous pages: The *Noisiel* wrecked at Prah Sands, Cornwall, in 1905

The *Gunvor* on the Lizard in 1912. The bowsprit is almost touching the rocks

The *Horsa* aground in the Scillies. She appears to have hit
gently and attempts are being made to get her off

The *Cromdale* on the Lizard in Cornwall

The *Cromdale* a few days after she struck.
All the masts but the fore have gone

The end of the *Cromdale*

Small boats clustered round the *Cromdale* shortly after she went aground. The rocks off the Lizard took many a ship as captains came in too close in order to get into Falmouth, or missed their way in fog

The *Falls of Halladale* the morning after she struck. She was trying to go about when she hit the rocks

The barque *Noel* well ashore at Bangor, North Wales, in 1887

Above: The *Pavo* ex *Glendovey* half-submerged on a sandbank in Montevideo Bay

The *Galatea* aground on Smith's Knoll, off Norfolk, in 1898

Left: Not all vessels stranded or put ashore were lost. In 1901 the *Loch Vennachar* was rammed while at anchor off Thames Haven, on the Essex bank of the Thames Estuary, by the S.S. *Cato* and sank in forty feet of water. No lives were lost and this photograph shows her being recovered by salvage craft. She was repaired

Perhaps one of the greatest dangers to seamen – the derelict. The *Lysglimt* ex *Pesca* ex *Blytheswood*, which had been abandoned by her crew for one reason or another, but had somehow failed to sink. Floating around the shipping lanes, sometimes almost submerged, derelicts presented an unlit hazard that could easily sink a vessel unlucky enough to strike her. Ships sighting derelicts usually stopped to identify and sink them

The *Emigrant* hard aground. The deck cargo of timber has shifted to
leeward

Below: Even in relatively calm conditions the sea keeps up its destructive work. Here the swell wave breaks over the main deck of the *Gifford*

Right: The French ship *Alice* wrecked on San Island at the mouth of the Columbia River

189

The end of the *Pindos* off the Lizard in 1912

INDEX